SHORT
PRAYERS
OF WISDOM
FOR
MEN

HARVEST HOUSE PUBLISHERS
EUGENE, OREGON

Short Prayers of Wisdom for Men
Copyright © 2021 by PLJ Communications
Published by Harvest House Publishers
Eugene, Oregon 97408
www.harvesthousepublishers.com

ISBN 978-0-7369-8206-1 (pbk.)
ISBN 978-0-7369-8207-8 (eBook)

Design by Peter Gloege | LOOK Design Studio

Printed in the United States of America
21 22 23 24 25 26 27 28 29 / VP / 10 9 8 7 6 5 4 3 2 1

CONTENTS

PRAYER

IS THE EXERCISE OF

DRAWING ON THE

GRACE OF GOD.

—OSWALD CHAMBERS

ILLUMINATE
MY MIND

BLESSED ARE THE POOR IN SPIRIT,
FOR THEIRS IS THE KINGDOM OF HEAVEN.

BLESSED ARE THOSE WHO MOURN,
FOR THEY WILL BE COMFORTED.

BLESSED ARE THE MEEK,
FOR THEY WILL INHERIT THE EARTH.

**BLESSED ARE THOSE WHO HUNGER
AND THIRST FOR RIGHTEOUSNESS,**
FOR THEY WILL BE FILLED.

BLESSED ARE THE MERCIFUL,
FOR THEY WILL BE SHOWN MERCY.

BLESSED ARE THE PURE IN HEART,
FOR THEY WILL SEE GOD.

BLESSED ARE THE PEACEMAKERS,
FOR THEY WILL BE CALLED CHILDREN OF GOD.

**BLESSED ARE THOSE WHO ARE
PERSECUTED BECAUSE OF RIGHTEOUSNESS,**
FOR THEIRS IS THE KINGDOM OF HEAVEN.

—JESUS CHRIST, MATTHEW 5:3-10

ALL-WISE GOD,

MAY I FIX WHAT IS BROKEN,
RETURN WHAT I BORROW,
CARE FOR WHAT I VALUE,
ASK FOR WHAT I NEED,
PROTECT WHAT IS FRAGILE,
HONOR WHAT IS SACRED.
MAY I SAY THE KIND WORD,
DO THE KIND ACT. ALWAYS,
AND REGARDLESS OF THE
CONSEQUENCES.

—PATRICK LAWRENCE

GOD TAUGHT ME

AS A SCHOOLTEACHER

TEACHES A PUPIL.

—SAINT IGNATIUS

POINT THE DIRECTION, LORD.

YOUR SERVANT IS READY

TO MOVE FORWARD.

AMEN

DEAR GOD,
I HAVE SO MANY
TROUBLES TODAY.
MAY I LEAVE THEM
WITH YOU?

———

THE WORLD IS CHARGED WITH THE
GRANDEUR OF GOD.

—GERARD MANLEY HOPKINS

I PRAY THAT THE EYES OF YOUR HEART
MAY BE ENLIGHTENED

IN ORDER THAT YOU MAY KNOW THE
HOPE TO WHICH HE HAS CALLED YOU,

THE RICHES OF HIS GLORIOUS
INHERITANCE IN HIS HOLY PEOPLE,

AND HIS INCOMPARABLY GREAT POWER
FOR US WHO BELIEVE.

**THAT POWER IS THE SAME
AS THE MIGHTY STRENGTH**

HE EXERTED WHEN HE RAISED CHRIST
FROM THE DEAD

AND SEATED HIM AT HIS RIGHT HAND
IN THE HEAVENLY REALMS.

—EPHESIANS 1:18-20

O GOD,

PLEASE SHOWER YOUR WISDOM
ON THOSE LIVING IN CONFUSION
AND DARKNESS,
AND YOUR PEACE OF MIND
ON ALL WHO ARE TROUBLED.
AMEN.

MAY THE HOLY SPIRIT
GUIDE US AS WE SEEK TO
HEAL AND NURTURE THE EARTH
AND ALL OF ITS CREATURES,
TO LIVE IN THE MIDST OF CREATION,
AND TO LOVE ONE ANOTHER
AS BROTHERS AND SISTERS
WITH ALL LIFE.

—U.N. ENVIRONMENTAL
SABBATH PROGRAM

WHEN YOU
DRAW CLOSE TO GOD,
GOD WILL
DRAW CLOSE TO YOU.

—JAMES 4:8 TLB

———

WE PRAISE THEE, O GOD,
FOR THY GLORY DISPLAYED
IN ALL THE CREATURES
OF THE EARTH....
THEY AFFIRM THEE IN LIVING;
ALL THINGS AFFIRM THEE IN LIVING.

—T.S. ELIOT
FROM THE PLAY *MURDER IN THE CATHEDRAL*, 1935

BEHOLD, LORD...
MY WORLD IS FILLING
WITH DARKNESS,
WITH IGNORANCE.
TODAY MAY I OFFER
**ALL OF THE
LIGHT AND TRUTH**
THAT I CAN. AMEN.

———

A GENEROUS PERSON
WILL BE BLESSED.

—PROVERBS 22:9 CSB

DEAR GOD,

WHEN I THINK IT'S OVER,

REMIND ME THAT IT'S NOT OVER.

AMEN.

.... ❧ ....

THE LIGHT OF GOD SURROUNDS ME;

THE LOVE OF GOD ENFOLDS ME;

THE POWER OF GOD PROTECTS ME;

THE PRESENCE OF GOD WATCHES OVER ME;

WHEREVER I AM, GOD IS.

—J.D. FREEMAN

DEAR GOD,
MAY I TREAT MY BODY,
MIND, AND SOUL
LIKE THEY BELONG
TO SOMEONE WHO
LOVES ME.
AMEN.

———

THE PRICE OF NOT LOVING OURSELVES

AS GOD LOVES US IS A PRICE

NO ONE SHOULD HAVE TO PAY.

—T.J. GORDON

BE PRAISED, MY LORD,

THROUGH THOSE WHO

FORGIVE FOR LOVE OF YOU;

THROUGH THOSE WHO ENDURE

SICKNESS AND TRIAL.

HAPPY ARE THOSE WHO

ENDURE IN PEACE,

FOR BY YOU, MOST HIGH,

THEY WILL BE CROWNED.

—SAINT FRANCIS OF ASSISI

BREATHE IN ME, O HOLY SPIRIT,

THAT MY THOUGHTS MAY ALL BE HOLY.

ACT IN ME, O HOLY SPIRIT,

THAT MY WORK, TOO, MAY BE HOLY.

DRAW MY HEART, O HOLY SPIRIT,

THAT I LOVE BUT WHAT IS HOLY.

STRENGTHEN ME, O HOLY SPIRIT,

TO DEFEND ALL THAT IS HOLY.

GUARD ME, THEN, O HOLY SPIRIT,

THAT I ALWAYS MAY BE HOLY.

—SAINT AUGUSTINE

LORD OF ALL,
THANK YOU FOR THE
SACRED PRIVILEGE OF
BEING ALIVE.
ALIVE TO LOVE, TO SERVE,
TO SHARE, TO REJOICE.
AMEN.

———

THE LARK'S ON THE WING;
THE SNAIL'S ON THE THORN:
GOD'S IN HIS HEAVEN—
ALL'S RIGHT WITH THE WORLD!

—ROBERT BROWNING

MY ALL-KNOWING
CREATOR,
TODAY MAY I CHOOSE
MY WORDS WITH LOVE AND CARE,
TODAY MAY I LIFT THE SPIRITS
OF ANY WHO GRIEVE, TODAY
MAY I BE WILLING TO FORGIVE,
AND TO ASK FORGIVENESS, TODAY
MAY I LEAD OTHERS,
AS YOU HAVE LED ME. AMEN.

—PATRICK LAWRENCE

LET US LEARN TO CAST OUR
HEARTS INTO GOD.

—SAINT BERNARD OF CLAIRVAUX

DEAR GOD,
NONE OF SELF,
AND
ALL OF THEE.
AMEN.

—THEODORE MONOD

GOD SHAPES THE
WORLD BY PRAYER.

—E.M. BOUNDS

YOU ARE A SHADE IN THE HEAT,

YOU ARE A SHELTER IN THE COLD,

YOU ARE EYES TO THE BLIND,

YOU ARE A STAFF TO THE PILGRIM,

YOU ARE AN ISLAND IN THE SEA,

YOU ARE A STRONGHOLD UPON THE LAND,

YOU ARE A WELL IN THE WASTELAND,

YOU ARE HEALING TO THE SICK.

YOU ARE THE LUCK OF EVERY JOY,

YOU ARE THE LIGHT OF THE SUN'S BEAMS,

YOU ARE THE DOOR OF LORDLY WELCOME,

YOU ARE THE POLESTAR OF GUIDANCE,

YOU ARE THE STEP OF THE ROE OF THE HEIGHT,

YOU ARE THE STEP OF THE WHITE-FACED MARE,

YOU ARE THE GRACE OF THE SWIMMING SWAN,

YOU ARE THE JEWEL IN EACH MYSTERY.

—GAELIC PRAYER

LOVE ALL
GOD'S CREATION,
BOTH THE WHOLE AND
EVERY GRAIN OF SAND.
LOVE EVERY LEAF,
EVERY RAY OF LIGHT.
LOVE THE ANIMALS,
LOVE THE PLANTS,
LOVE EACH
SEPARATE THING.
IF THOU LOVE EACH THING,
THOU WILT PERCEIVE
THE MYSTERY OF GOD
IN ALL.

—FYODOR DOSTOEVSKY

THANK YOU, LORD JESUS,
FOR YOUR WORD,
WHICH INSTRUCTS ME
TO LIVE A LIFE OF WISDOM
AND THOUGHTFULNESS
AND REAL JOY.
AMEN.

NEVER STOP PRAYING.

—1 THESSALONIANS 5:17 NLT

O THOU, WHO ART WISDOM AND PITY BOTH,
SET ME FREE FROM THE LORDSHIP OF DESIRE.
HELP ME TO FIND MY HAPPINESS IN WHAT
IS MY ACCEPTANCE OF THY PURPOSE FOR ME:
IN FRIENDLY EYES: IN WORK WELL DONE:
IN QUIETNESS BORN OF TRUST,
AND, MOST OF ALL, IN THE AWARENESS
OF THY PRESENCE IN MY SPIRIT.

—ALISTAIR MACLEAN

CONCENTRATE ON COUNTING YOUR BLESSINGS, AND YOU'LL HAVE LITTLE TIME TO COUNT ANYTHING ELSE.

—WOODROW KROLL

FATHER GOD,
MY MIND IS TROUBLED
AND CONFUSED.
I WANT TO REST.
I WANT TO TURN ALL
OF MY THOUGHTS
TO YOU. PLEASE
HELP ME DO THIS.
AMEN.

NOW IS YOUR TIME OF GRIEF,

BUT I WILL SEE YOU AGAIN

AND YOU WILL REJOICE,

AND NO ONE WILL TAKE AWAY

YOUR JOY.

—JOHN 16:22

LIFE IS PRECIOUS,

AND THE UNEXPECTED WILL HAPPEN.

THESE TWO TRUTHS GIVE US GOOD REASON

TO BE AS READY AS WE CAN.

—T.J. GORDON

DEAR GOD,

PLEASE GRANT ME

THE COURAGE & THE STRENGTH

TO WALK THE GOOD ROAD,

NO MATTER HOW NARROW OR

STEEP OR HARD IT MAY BE.

AMEN.

—TAYLOR MORGAN

TEACH ME,
AND I WILL BE QUIET;
SHOW ME WHERE
I HAVE BEEN WRONG.

—JOB 6:24

❧

IT IS GOOD TO **LOVE** MANY THINGS,

FOR THEREIN LIES STRENGTH,

AND WHOSOEVER **LOVES** MUCH

PERFORMS MUCH,

AND CAN ACCOMPLISH MUCH,

AND WHAT IS DONE WITH **LOVE**

IS WELL DONE.

—VINCENT VAN GOGH

HEAVENLY FATHER,

YOUR WILL, NOT MY WILL, BE DONE.

HARD WORDS FOR ME TO PRAY.

BUT I MEAN THEM.

AMEN.

———

IF GOD SENDS YOU DOWN A STONY PATH, MAY HE GIVE YOU STRONG SHOES.

—CELTIC BLESSING

HEAVENLY FATHER,

I KNOW YOU ARE REAL.

HELP ME, AS I PRAY,

TO BE REAL WITH YOU.

AMEN.

—PATRICK LAWRENCE

WE ARE HIS WORKMANSHIP,

CREATED IN CHRIST JESUS

FOR GOOD WORKS,

WHICH GOD PREPARED AHEAD OF TIME

FOR US TO DO.

—EPHESIANS 2:10 CSB

DEAR JESUS, TODAY MAY I CHOOSE WISDOM. AMEN.

———

IT'S WHAT YOU'VE LEARNED AFTER YOU KNOW IT ALL THAT COUNTS.

—COACH JOHN WOODEN

I WATCH IN HOPE FOR YOU, LORD;

I WAIT ON GOD MY SAVIOR,

AND I KNOW YOU HEAR ME

WHEN I PRAY. THANK YOU.

—INSPIRED BY MICAH 7:7

GOD DOES NOT GIVE US EVERYTHING WE WANT,

BUT HE DOES FULFILL HIS PROMISES,

LEADING US ALONG THE BEST AND STRAIGHTEST

PATHS TO HIMSELF.

—DIETRICH BONHOEFFER

TO PRAY IS TO OPEN
YOUR WHOLE SELF TO LOVE, TO TRUTH, TO THE LIFE YOU WERE DESTINED TO LIVE.

—PATRICK LAWRENCE

I PRAY FOR MERCY FOR ALL THOSE WHO HUNGER FOR IT. PLEASE COMFORT THOSE WHO SUFFER FROM INJUSTICE; SHELTER THEM IN THE FORTRESS OF YOUR LOVE. HELP YOUR PEOPLE TURN THEIR EYES AND EARS AND HEARTS TOWARD THOSE IN NEED. GIVE US COURAGE TO ACT NOW. WE PRAY TO YOU AND RELY ON YOUR COMPASSION; WE COME TO YOU AND RELY ON YOUR LOVE. AMEN.

—T.J. GORDON

DEAR JESUS,

OPEN MY EYES TO SEE
THE NEEDS OF OTHERS;

OPEN MY EARS SO THAT
I CAN HEAR THEIR CRIES;

OPEN MY HEART AND
HELP ME TO FEED THE HUNGRY,
DEFEND THE WEAK, AND BRING
PEACE TO THE TROUBLED.

AMEN.

—TAYLOR MORGAN

HOW PRECIOUS ARE YOUR
THOUGHTS ABOUT ME, O GOD.
THEY CANNOT BE NUMBERED!
I CAN'T EVEN COUNT THEM;
THEY OUTNUMBER THE GRAINS
OF SAND. THANK YOU FOR
THINKING ABOUT ME. AMEN.

—INSPIRED BY PSALM 139

EVEN IN DARKNESS
LIGHT DAWNS FOR THE UPRIGHT,
FOR THOSE WHO ARE GRACIOUS
AND COMPASSIONATE AND RIGHTEOUS.

—PSALM 112:4

DEAR GOD,

I ENTRUST TO YOU MY NEEDS,

AS WELL AS THE NEEDS OF THOSE I LOVE.

IN A WORLD WHERE MANY SHADOWS LURK,

MAY YOUR WISDOM AND TRUTH

LIGHT OUR WAY. AMEN.

LOVE WILL
TAKE YOU PLACES
THE MIND
CAN'T SEE.

—CRAIG SAGER

HEAVENLY FATHER,

RIGHT NOW, I SEND PRAYERS OF THANKS

FOR ALL PEOPLE AROUND THE WORLD

WHO ARE GIVING OF THEMSELVES,

GIVING THEIR BEST FOR YOUR CREATION.

AMEN.

· · · · · · · · · ❧ · · · · · · · · ·

WHEN I APPROACH THE LORD

IN PRAYER,

I FEEL HIS LIFE AND HIS LOVE.

I FEEL A WORLD BEING REBORN.

—BRYCE DONOVAN

CREATOR GOD,

I THANK YOU THAT I AM ALIVE

BECAUSE YOU GAVE ME BREATH.

AND I THANK YOU FOR DOING THIS

BECAUSE YOU LOVE ME.

AMEN.

—TAYLOR MORGAN

OUR JOB IS TO LOVE OTHERS
WITHOUT STOPPING
TO INQUIRE WHETHER OR NOT

THEY ARE WORTHY. THAT IS NOT

OUR BUSINESS AND, IN FACT,

IT IS NOBODY'S BUSINESS.

WHAT WE ARE ASKED TO DO IS TO

LOVE, AND THIS LOVE ITSELF

WILL RENDER BOTH OURSELVES

AND OUR NEIGHBORS WORTHY

IF ANYTHING CAN.

—THOMAS MERTON

HEAVENLY FATHER,
PLEASE GIVE ME THE HOPE AND THE COURAGE
TO BEGIN THE NEW THING THAT MY SOUL
YEARNS TO DO. AMEN.

IF YOU DO NOT HOPE,
YOU WILL NOT FIND WHAT IS
BEYOND YOUR HOPES.

—SAINT CLEMENT OF ALEXANDRIA

LORD,

SOMEHOW, SOME WAY,

MAY I BE A SOURCE OF COMFORT

AND STRENGTH TO SOMEONE TODAY.

IN YOUR NAME I PRAY.

—INSPIRED BY HAGGAI 1:7

———

DON'T FORGET TO PRAY TODAY,

BECAUSE GOD DID NOT FORGET

TO WAKE YOU UP THIS MORNING.

—OSWALD CHAMBERS

WHERE YOUR PLEASURE IS,

THERE IS YOUR TREASURE.

WHERE YOUR TREASURE IS,

THERE IS YOUR HEART.

WHERE YOUR HEART IS,

THERE IS YOUR HAPPINESS.

—SAINT AUGUSTINE

THIS IS WHAT THE LORD,
THE GOD OF YOUR
FATHER DAVID, SAYS:
I HAVE HEARD YOUR
PRAYER
AND SEEN YOUR TEARS;
I WILL HEAL YOU.

—2 KINGS 20:5

LORD GOD,

THANK YOU FOR TEACHING US
TO PRAY, AND FOR PROMISING
TO HEAR THE UNITED VOICES
OF TWO OR THREE OF YOUR
CHILDREN CALLING YOUR NAME.
HEAR NOW THE PRAYERS
OF YOUR SERVANTS. GIVE US
IN THIS WORLD KNOWLEDGE
OF YOUR HEAVENLY TRUTH,
AND IN THE WORLD TO COME,
THE HEAVENLY LIFE EVERLASTING.
IN THE NAME OF CHRIST OUR LORD,

AMEN.

—INSPIRED BY A FOURTH-CENTURY
ARMENIAN LITURGY

GUIDE
MY STEPS

GOD

IS STRIDING AHEAD OF YOU.

HE'S RIGHT THERE WITH YOU.

HE WON'T LET YOU DOWN;

HE WON'T LEAVE YOU.

DON'T BE INTIMIDATED.

DON'T WORRY.

—DEUTERONOMY 31:8 MSG

BEWARE IN YOUR PRAYERS, ABOVE
EVERYTHING ELSE, OF LIMITING GOD,
NOT ONLY BY UNBELIEF, BUT BY
FANCYING THAT YOU KNOW WHAT
HE CAN DO.

**EXPECT UNEXPECTED THINGS….
EACH TIME, BEFORE YOU INTERCEDE,
BE QUIET FIRST, AND WORSHIP GOD
IN HIS GLORY.**

THINK OF WHAT HE CAN DO, AND
HOW HE DELIGHTS TO HEAR THE
PRAYERS OF HIS REDEEMED PEOPLE.

**THINK OF YOUR PLACE AND
PRIVILEGE IN CHRIST, AND EXPECT
GREAT THINGS!**

— ANDREW MURRAY

DEAR GOD,

MAY I LEARN

FROM EVERY FAILURE,

MINE AND

THOSE OF OTHERS.

AMEN.

———

ABOVE ALL ELSE,

GUARD YOUR HEART,

FOR EVERYTHING YOU DO

FLOWS FROM IT.

—PROVERBS 4:23

LORD,

THANK YOU FOR ASSURING ME THAT MY CURRENT PREDICAMENT IS NOT MY FINAL DESTINATION.

TRIALS TEACH US WHAT WE ARE;

THEY DIG UP THE SOIL AND LET US SEE

WHAT WE ARE MADE OF.

—CHARLES SPURGEON

> ## WE ARE MIRRORS OF GOD, CREATED TO REFLECT HIM.
>
> —PHILIP YANCEY

ALONE WITH NONE BUT THEE, MY GOD,

I JOURNEY ON MY WAY.

WHAT NEED I FEAR WHEN THOU ART NEAR,

OH KING OF NIGHT AND DAY?

MORE SAFE AM I WITHIN THY HAND

THAN IF A HOST DID ROUND ME STAND.

—SAINT COLUMBA

HOLY MAKER OF ALL THINGS,

MAKE MY LIFE AN OFFERING;

MAKE MY LIFE A PRAYER. AMEN.

❧

MY CREATOR,
I CHERISH YOU FOR REVEALING TO ME
THE PATH OF LIFE.
I PRAISE YOU FOR FILLING ME
WITH JOY IN YOUR PRESENCE.
I THANK YOU FOR THE LOVING GIFTS
OF YOUR RIGHTEOUS RIGHT HAND.
AMEN.

—INSPIRED BY PSALM 16:11

WALK WITH THE WISE

AND BECOME WISE.

—PROVERBS 13:20

———

I HAVE SO MUCH TO DO

THAT I SHALL HAVE TO SPEND

THE FIRST THREE HOURS

IN PRAYER.

—MARTIN LUTHER

HEAVENLY FATHER,
PLEASE BRING JOY TO MY HEART
SO THAT I CAN SHARE JOY WITH OTHERS.
AMEN.

———

HOW FAR YOU GO IN LIFE DEPENDS ON

YOUR BEING TENDER WITH THE YOUNG,

COMPASSIONATE WITH THE AGED,

SYMPATHETIC WITH THE STRIVING,

AND TOLERANT OF THE WEAK AND STRONG.

BECAUSE SOMEDAY IN LIFE,

YOU WILL HAVE BEEN ALL OF THESE.

—GEORGE WASHINGTON CARVER

IN THIS WORLD,
IT IS NOT WHAT WE TAKE UP,
BUT WHAT WE GIVE UP,
THAT MAKES US RICH.

—HENRY WARD BEECHER

DEAR GOD, MAY I ALWAYS
REMEMBER THAT **LOVE**
NEVER GIVES UP, AND
THAT **LOVE** CARES FOR OTHERS
MORE THAN SELF. **AMEN.**

—INSPIRED BY
1 CORINTHIANS 13:4

LOOK UPON US, O LORD,

AND LET THE DARKNESS

OF OUR SOULS

VANISH BEFORE THE BEAMS

OF THY BRIGHTNESS.

FILL US WITH HOLY LOVE,

AND OPEN TO US THE TREASURES

OF THY WISDOM.

ALL OUR DESIRE IS KNOWN

UNTO THEE;

THEREFORE PERFECT WHAT

THOU HAST BEGUN,

AND WHAT THY SPIRIT HAS

AWAKENED US TO ASK IN PRAYER.

WE SEEK THY FACE;

TURN THY FACE UNTO US

AND SHOW US THY GLORY.

THEN SHALL OUR LONGING

BE SATISFIED, AND OUR

PEACE SHALL BE PERFECT.

—SAINT AUGUSTINE

A PRESIDENTIAL PRAYER

O ETERNAL AND EVERLASTING GOD,
I PRESUME TO PRESENT MYSELF THIS MORNING
BEFORE THY DIVINE MAJESTY,
BESEECHING THEE TO ACCEPT OF MY
HUMBLE AND HEARTY THANKS,
THAT IT HATH PLEASED THY GREAT GOODNESS
TO KEEP AND PRESERVE ME THE NIGHT PAST
FROM ALL THE DANGERS POOR MORTALS
ARE SUBJECT TO, AND HAS GIVEN ME
SWEET AND PLEASANT SLEEP,
WHEREBY I FIND MY BODY REFRESHED
AND COMFORTED FOR PERFORMING
THE DUTIES OF THIS DAY, IN WHICH
I BESEECH THEE TO DEFEND ME FROM
ALL PERILS OF BODY AND SOUL.

—GEORGE WASHINGTON

NO MAN IS GREATER THAN HIS PRAYER LIFE.

—LEONARD RAVENHILL

TRUST IN THE LORD
WITH ALL YOUR HEART,
AND DO NOT RELY ON YOUR
OWN UNDERSTANDING;
IN ALL YOUR WAYS KNOW HIM,
AND HE WILL MAKE YOUR
PATHS STRAIGHT.

—PROVERBS 3:5-6 CSB

IN A CULTURE INCREASINGLY RULED BY
CONFLICT AND POLARIZATION,
TEACH US WHAT IT WOULD MEAN AND
COST FOR US TO FOLLOW JESUS, WHO SAYS,

"BLESSED ARE THE PEACEMAKERS,
FOR THEY SHALL BE CALLED
THE CHILDREN OF GOD."

LORD, HELP US TO FIND THE STRENGTH TO BE
THOSE CHILDREN OF GOD WHO SHOW LOVE
AND NOT CONTEMPT FOR OUR ENEMIES AND SEEK TO
RESOLVE OUR DEEPENING CONFLICTS.

—JOHN LEWIS

GIVE US, LORD, A BIT OF SUN,
A BIT OF WORK, AND A BIT OF FUN;

GIVE US IN ALL THE STRUGGLE AND SPUTTER
OUR DAILY BREAD, A BIT OF BUTTER.

GIVE US HEALTH, OUR KEEP TO MAKE
AND A BIT TO SPARE, FOR OTHERS' SAKE.

GIVE US, TOO, A BIT OF SONG,
AND A TALE AND A BOOK TO HELP US ALONG.

GIVE US, LORD, A CHANCE TO BE
OUR GOODLY BEST—BRAVE, WISE, AND FREE.
OUR GOODLY BEST FOR OURSELVES AND OTHERS,
LEARNING TO LIVE AS SISTERS AND BROTHERS.

—OLD ENGLISH PRAYER

LEAD US, O GOD,

FROM THE SIGHT OF THE LOVELY THINGS
OF THE WORLD TO THE THOUGHT OF THEE,

THEIR CREATOR;

AND GRANT THAT IN DELIGHTING IN THE
BEAUTIFUL THINGS OF THY CREATION,
WE MAY DELIGHT IN THEE, THE FIRST AUTHOR
OF BEAUTY AND THE SOVEREIGN LORD
OF ALL THY WORKS, BLESSED FOR EVERMORE.

— SAINT THOMAS AQUINAS

WE CAN NEVER KNOW
WHO WE ARE
UNTIL WE KNOW
AT LEAST SOMETHING
OF WHAT GOD IS.

— A.W. TOZER

PRAYER
IS NOT ELOQUENCE,
BUT EARNESTNESS.

—HANNAH MORE

THANK YOU, LORD, FOR ALWAYS . . .
GUIDING MY STEPS,
CLEARING MY MIND,
HEALING MY HEART,
AND RESTORING MY SOUL.
AMEN.

MAY GOD'S BLESSINGS BE YOUR
CONSTANT COMPANIONS.

MAY HIS GRACE AND PEACE ABOUND
IN YOUR BODY AND SOUL.

MAY HIS LOVE SURROUND YOU.

MAY YOU WALK SOFTLY UPON
HOLY GROUND.

—PATRICK LAWRENCE

PRAYER WILL MAKE
A MAN CEASE FROM SIN,
OR SIN WILL ENTICE A MAN
TO CEASE FROM PRAYER.

—JOHN BUNYAN

DEAR LORD,
HELP ME TO FACE FEAR WISELY.
REMIND ME THAT
I CANNOT CONQUER FEAR
WITHOUT FIRST ACKNOWLEDGING IT.
IF I HAD NO FEARS,
I WOULDN'T KNOW WHAT
GODLY COURAGE IS.

—T.J. GORDON

TROUBLES ARE OFTEN THE TOOLS
BY WHICH GOD FASHIONS US
FOR BETTER THINGS.

—HENRY WARD BEECHER

FATHER,
PLEASE GUIDE ME ALWAYS
AND SATISFY MY NEEDS
IN A SUN-SCORCHED LAND.
PLEASE STRENGTHEN MY FRAME.
MAKE ME LIKE A WELL-WATERED GARDEN,
LIKE A SPRING WHOSE WATERS
NEVER FAIL. AMEN.

—INSPIRED BY ISAIAH 58:11

JESUS, IN YOU ALONE
MY MIND FINDS PEACE,
MY BODY FINDS COMFORT,
MY SOUL FINDS REST.
AMEN.

"I KNOW THE PLANS
I HAVE FOR YOU,"
DECLARES THE LORD,
"PLANS TO PROSPER YOU
AND NOT HARM YOU,
PLANS TO GIVE YOU
HOPE AND A FUTURE."

—JEREMIAH 29:11

HEAVENLY FATHER,

GRANT ME THE COURAGE TO SPEAK

WHEN OTHERS NEED TO HEAR ME

AND THE PATIENCE TO LISTEN

WHEN OTHERS NEED TO SPEAK TO ME.

GIVE ME WISDOM TO SERVE THE WISE

AND ENDURANCE TO SERVE THE UNWISE.

PLEASE SAVE ME FROM TOO MUCH WORK

AND REFRESH ME WITH THE TONIC OF REST.

AMEN.

—PATRICK LAWRENCE

HEAVENLY FATHER,
RIGHT NOW, I DON'T WANT TO
ASK YOU FOR ANYTHING.
I JUST WANT TO THANK YOU
FOR ALL YOU HAVE DONE
FOR ME. AMEN.

IT'S NOT HOW MUCH WE HAVE,
BUT HOW MUCH WE ENJOY
THAT MAKES HAPPINESS.

—CHARLES SPURGEON

HEAVENLY FATHER,

PLEASE KEEP MY EYES OPEN

AND MY HEART PURE.

AMEN.

———

CARVE A TUNNEL
OF HOPE
THROUGH THE
DARK MOUNTAIN
OF DESPAIR.

—MARTIN LUTHER KING JR.

MERCIFUL GOD,
HELP ME TO REMEMBER
THAT THE PEOPLE
WHO ARE HARDEST
FOR ME TO LOVE
ARE OFTEN THE ONES
WHO NEED MY LOVE
THE MOST.

BE COMPLETELY
HUMBLE AND GENTLE;
BE PATIENT, BEARING WITH
ONE ANOTHER IN LOVE.

—EPHESIANS 4:2

LORD, LET ME BE
THE REASON
SOMEONE STILL BELIEVES IN
HONESTY AND INTEGRITY.
AMEN.

PRAYER
IS KEEPING
COMPANY
WITH GOD.

—CLEMENT OF ALEXANDRIA

GOD,
I HOPE THAT I CAN DO
SOMETHING TODAY
THAT MAKES YOU SMILE.
AMEN.

GO AFTER A LIFE OF LOVE

AS IF YOUR LIFE DEPENDED ON IT—
BECAUSE IT DOES. GIVE YOURSELVES TO
THE GIFTS GOD GIVES YOU.

—1 CORINTHIANS 14:1 MSG

DEAR JESUS,
MAY I FACE TODAY
WITH AN
OPEN HEART,
NOT A CLOSED MIND.
AMEN.

⚜

THE LORD IS NEAR. DO NOT BE ANXIOUS
ABOUT ANYTHING, BUT IN EVERY SITUATION,
BY PRAYER AND PETITION, WITH THANKSGIVING,
PRESENT YOUR REQUESTS TO GOD.
AND THE PEACE OF GOD,
WHICH TRANSCENDS ALL UNDERSTANDING,
WILL GUARD YOUR HEARTS AND YOUR MINDS
IN CHRIST JESUS.

—PHILIPPIANS 4:5-7

HEAVENLY FATHER,

I WANT TO LEAVE EVERYTHING BETTER

THAN WHEN I FOUND IT—ESPECIALLY

THE LOST, THE BROKEN, AND THE LONELY.

PLEASE HELP ME DO THIS. AMEN.

———

HOPE IS THE POWER OF
BEING CHEERFUL
IN CIRCUMSTANCES WHICH
WE KNOW TO BE DESPERATE.

—G.K. CHESTERTON

NOW TO HIM WHO IS ABLE TO DO

IMMEASURABLY MORE

THAN ALL WE ASK OR IMAGINE,

ACCORDING TO HIS POWER

THAT IS AT WORK WITHIN US,

TO HIM BE GLORY IN THE CHURCH

AND IN CHRIST JESUS

THROUGHOUT ALL GENERATIONS,

FOR EVER AND EVER! AMEN.

—EPHESIANS 3:20-21

INTO THY HANDS, O LORD,

AND INTO THE HANDS OF THY HOLY ANGELS,

I COMMIT AND ENTRUST THIS DAY MY SOUL,

MY RELATIONS, MY BENEFACTORS, MY FRIENDS,

AND MY ENEMIES, AND ALL THY PEOPLE.

KEEP US, O LORD, THROUGH THIS DAY.

—SAINT EDMUND OF ABINGDON

FINALLY, BRETHREN,
  WHATSOEVER THINGS ARE TRUE,
  WHATSOEVER THINGS ARE HONEST,
  WHATSOEVER THINGS ARE JUST,
  WHATSOEVER THINGS ARE PURE,
  WHATSOEVER THINGS ARE LOVELY,
  WHATSOEVER THINGS ARE OF GOOD REPORT;

IF THERE BE ANY VIRTUE,
  AND IF THERE BE ANY PRAISE,
  THINK ON THESE THINGS.

—PHILIPPIANS 4:8 KJV

A PRAYER FOR YOU

COMFORT ON HARD DAYS,

SMILES WHEN SADNESS INVADES,

RAINBOWS TO FOLLOW STORM CLOUDS,

KINDNESS TO KISS YOUR CHEEK,

SUNSETS TO CALM YOUR SPIRIT,

HUGS WHEN YOUR HEART GROWS HEAVY,

BEAUTY FOR ALL YOUR SENSES,

FRIENDSHIP TO ENRICH YOUR DAYS,

FAITH TO LIGHT THE WAY,

REASSURANCE WHEN YOU FEAR,

COURAGE TO KNOW YOURSELF,

PATIENCE TO ACCEPT TRUTH,

LOVE TO MAKE LIFE COMPLETE.

—RALPH WALDO EMERSON

O LORD MY GOD,

TEACH MY HEART THIS DAY
WHERE AND HOW TO SEE YOU,
WHERE AND HOW TO FIND YOU.
YOU HAVE MADE ME AND REMADE ME,
AND YOU HAVE BESTOWED ON ME
ALL THE GOOD THINGS I POSSESS,
AND STILL I DO NOT KNOW YOU.
I HAVE NOT YET DONE THAT
FOR WHICH I WAS MADE.
TEACH ME TO SEEK YOU,
FOR I CANNOT SEEK YOU
UNLESS YOU TEACH ME, OR FIND YOU
UNLESS YOU SHOW YOURSELF TO ME.
LET ME SEEK YOU IN MY DESIRE,
LET ME DESIRE YOU IN MY SEEKING.
LET ME FIND YOU BY LOVING YOU,
LET ME LOVE YOU WHEN I FIND YOU.

—SAINT ANSELM

MAY GOD THE FATHER
BLESS US,

MAY CHRIST
TAKE CARE OF US,

THE HOLY GHOST
ENLIGHTEN US

ALL THE DAYS OF OUR LIFE.
THE LORD BE OUR DEFENDER
AND KEEPER OF BODY AND SOUL,
BOTH NOW AND FOREVER,
TO THE AGES OF AGES.

—SAINT ÆTHELWOLD

———

PRAISE BE TO YOU, LORD;
TEACH ME YOUR DECREES.

—PSALM 119:12

BE STRONG AND COURAGEOUS, AND ACT;
DO NOT FEAR NOR BE DISMAYED,
FOR THE LORD GOD, MY GOD,
IS WITH YOU. HE WILL NOT FAIL YOU
NOR FORSAKE YOU.

—1 CHRONICLES 28:20 NASB

EVERY GREAT MOVEMENT OF GOD CAN BE TRACED TO A KNEELING FIGURE.

—DWIGHT L. MOODY

FORWARD

I GO WITH YOU, LORD,

THE ONE WHO HOLDS MY HEART.

ONE STEP AT A TIME,

ONE BREATH AT A TIME,

ONE MOMENT AT A TIME.

AMEN.

THE JOURNEY TOWARD WISDOM
SHOULD NEVER BE ATTEMPTED WITHOUT
A HEALTHY SUPPLY OF HUMILITY.

—BRYCE DONOVAN

A BLESSING FOR YOU

MAY YOU LIVE A LIFE WORTHY OF OUR LORD.

MAY YOU PLEASE HIM EVERY DAY, AS YOU DO GOOD
THINGS AND LEARN MORE AND MORE ABOUT GOD
AND HIS AMAZING SON.

MAY HE GIVE YOU STRENGTH AND ENDURANCE.

MAY YOU GIVE JOYFUL THANKS ALWAYS TO THE ONE
WHO HAS LET YOU ENTER THE KINGDOM OF LIGHT.

—INSPIRED BY COLOSSIANS 1:10-12

TAKE CARE! PROTECT YOURSELF
AGAINST THE LEAST BIT OF GREED.
LIFE IS NOT DEFINED
BY WHAT YOU HAVE,
EVEN WHEN YOU HAVE A LOT.

—LUKE 12:15 MSG

DEAR GOD,
WHEN LIFE PUSHES ME
TOWARD YET ANOTHER STORM,
PLEASE PULL ME BACK
INTO YOUR PEACE. AMEN.

I AM SURE OF THIS,

THAT HE WHO STARTED
A GOOD WORK IN YOU

WILL CARRY IT ON TO COMPLETION

UNTIL THE DAY OF CHRIST JESUS.

—PHILIPPIANS 1:6 CSB

THE PRAYER
OF A RIGHTEOUS PERSON
IS POWERFUL
AND EFFECTIVE.

—JAMES 5:16

———

CHARACTER
IS POWER.

—BOOKER T. WASHINGTON

RESTORE
MY SOUL

THE LONELY DAYS,

THE LONELY SEASONS OF LIFE,

ARE OFTEN

GOD'S WAYS OF SAYING,

"I WANT TO SPEND

MORE TIME WITH YOU;

I WANT TO RESTORE YOUR SOUL."

—PATRICK LAWRENCE

I DO NOT KNOW YOU, GOD,

BECAUSE I AM IN THE WAY.

PLEASE HELP ME

TO PUSH MYSELF ASIDE.

—FLANNERY O'CONNOR

TO LOVE OR NOT;

IN THIS WE STAND OR FALL.

—JOHN MILTON

GIVE PERFECTION TO BEGINNERS, O FATHER;

GIVE INTELLIGENCE TO THE LITTLE ONES;

GIVE AID TO THOSE WHO ARE RUNNING THEIR COURSE.

GIVE SORROW TO THE NEGLIGENT;

GIVE FERVOR OF THE SPIRIT TO THE LUKEWARM,

FOR THE SAKE OF CHRIST JESUS OUR LORD.

AMEN.

—SAINT IRENAEUS

ANYTHING IS A **BLESSING** WHICH MAKES US PRAY.

—CHARLES SPURGEON

FATHER GOD,

I PLACE MY LIFE IN YOUR HANDS,

BECAUSE I WANT TO SEE YOUR

HAND IN MY LIFE.

AMEN.

·········· ❧ ··········

CALL FOR HELP WHEN
YOU'RE IN TROUBLE—I'LL HELP YOU,
AND YOU'LL HONOR ME.

—PSALM 50:15 MSG

IN ME THERE IS DARKNESS,

BUT WITH THEE THERE IS LIGHT.

I AM LONELY, BUT THOU LEAVEST ME NOT.

**I AM FEEBLE IN HEART,
BUT THOU LEAVEST ME NOT.**

I AM RESTLESS, BUT WITH THEE THERE IS PEACE.

IN ME THERE IS BITTERNESS,

BUT WITH THEE THERE IS PATIENCE.

THY WAYS ARE PAST UNDERSTANDING,

BUT THOU KNOWEST THE WAY FOR ME.

—DIETRICH BONHOEFFER

LET MY PARCHED SOUL
DRINK IN YOUR PEACE,
O GOD. AMEN.

LET THE PEACE OF CHRIST
RULE IN YOUR HEARTS,
SINCE AS MEMBERS OF ONE BODY
YOU WERE CALLED TO PEACE.

—COLOSSIANS 3:15

JESUS,
MY FEET ARE DIRTY.

COME EVEN AS A SLAVE TO ME,

POUR WATER INTO YOUR BOWL,

COME & WASH MY FEET.

IN ASKING SUCH A THING

I KNOW I AM OVERBOLD,

BUT I READ WHAT WAS THREATENED

WHEN YOU SAID TO ME,

"IF I DO NOT WASH YOUR FEET

I HAVE NO FELLOWSHIP WITH YOU."

WASH MY FEET THEN, BECAUSE I LONG

FOR YOUR COMPANIONSHIP.

—ORIGEN

YOU CALLED AND CRIED TO ME

AND BROKE UPON MY DEAFNESS;

AND YOU SENT FORTH YOUR LIGHT

AND SHONE UPON ME,

AND CHASED AWAY MY BLINDNESS;

YOU BREATHED FRAGRANCE

UPON ME, AND I DREW IN MY BREATH

AND DID NOT PANT FOR YOU;

YOU TOUCHED ME,

AND I HAVE BURNED FOR YOUR PEACE.

—SAINT AUGUSTINE

BEFORE THE ENDING OF THE DAY,
CREATOR OF THE WORLD,

WE PRAY THAT THOU,

WITH WONTED LOVE,
WOULDST KEEP THY WATCH
AROUND US WHILE WE SLEEP.

—SAINT AMBROSE

———

BE JOYFUL IN HOPE,
PATIENT IN AFFLICTION,
FAITHFUL IN PRAYER.

—ROMANS 12:12

HEAVENLY FATHER,

WHEN IT SEEMS YOU ARE SILENT,
HELP ME TO REMEMBER THAT SILENCE
IS NOT NECESSARILY EMPTY.

**SILENCE CAN BE FULL OF INSIGHT,
CLARITY, AND PEACE.**

I THANK YOU FOR THE BLESSING
OF SILENCE. AMEN.

—TAYLOR MORGAN

SHINE INTO OUR HEARTS,
O LORD, WITH YOUR PURE LIGHT.

OPEN OUR MINDS TO
CONTEMPLATE YOUR TEACHINGS;
PLACE INTO US RESPECT FOR
YOUR BLESSED COMMANDMENTS.

MAY WE AVOID THE ROADS THAT
LEAD TO MEDIOCRITY OR SIN.

LEAD US TO THE HIGH ROAD,
THE ONE THAT LEADS TO A
RICH LIFE IN YOUR SPIRIT.

LET ALL WE THINK AND DO MEET
WITH YOUR GOOD PLEASURE.

FOR YOU ARE OUR LIGHT AND
OUR SALVATION.

TO YOU WE RENDER GLORY,
NOW AND FOREVER, AMEN.

—T.J. GORDON

PRAYER REQUIRES

MORE OF THE HEART
THAN OF THE TONGUE.

—ADAM CLARKE

LORD JESUS,

TODAY MAY I DISCOVER THE FREEDOM
OF REFUSING TO WORRY OR STRESS
ABOUT WHAT OTHER PEOPLE THINK.
AMEN.

TRUST IN HIM

AT ALL TIMES, YOU PEOPLE;
POUR OUT YOUR HEARTS TO HIM,
FOR GOD IS OUR REFUGE.

—PSALM 62:8

GOD OF MERCY,
I AM TRULY GRATEFUL
THAT YOUR GRACE
IS ALWAYS BIGGER
THAN MY SIN.
AMEN.

BEHOLD, LORD, AN EMPTY VESSEL
THAT NEEDS TO BE FILLED.

MY LORD, FILL IT. I AM WEAK IN THE FAITH;
STRENGTHEN ME. I AM COLD IN LOVE;
WARM ME AND MAKE ME FERVENT, THAT MY
LOVE MAY GO OUT TO MY NEIGHBOR.

I DO NOT HAVE A STRONG AND FIRM FAITH;
AT TIMES I DOUBT AND AM UNABLE TO TRUST
YOU ALTOGETHER.

O LORD, HELP ME. STRENGTHEN MY FAITH
AND TRUST IN YOU.

IN YOU I HAVE SEALED THE **TREASURE** OF ALL I HAVE. I AM POOR; YOU ARE RICH AND CAME TO BE **MERCIFUL** TO THE POOR. I AM A SINNER; YOU ARE UPRIGHT.

WITH ME, THERE IS AN ABUNDANCE OF SIN; IN YOU IS THE FULLNESS OF RIGHTEOUSNESS.

THEREFORE, I WILL REMAIN WITH YOU, OF WHOM I CAN **RECEIVE**, BUT TO WHOM I MAY NOT **GIVE**.

—MARTIN LUTHER

OUR PRAYER OF THANKS

FOR THE GLADNESS HERE WHERE
THE SUN IS SHINING AT EVENING
ON THE WEEDS AT THE RIVER,
OUR PRAYER OF THANKS.

FOR THE LAUGHTER OF CHILDREN
WHO TUMBLE BAREFOOTED AND
BAREHEADED IN THE SUMMER GRASS,
OUR PRAYER OF THANKS.

FOR THE SUNSET AND THE STARS,
THE WOMEN AND THE. . .
ARMS THAT HOLD US,
OUR PRAYER OF THANKS.

—CARL SANDBURG

THOSE WHO
HOPE IN THE LORD
WILL RENEW THEIR STRENGTH.

THEY WILL SOAR
ON WINGS LIKE EAGLES;

THEY WILL RUN
AND NOT GROW WEARY,

THEY WILL WALK
AND NOT BE FAINT.

—ISAIAH 40:31

IN **PEACE** I WILL
LIE DOWN AND SLEEP,
FOR YOU ALONE,
LORD,
MAKE ME DWELL
IN **SAFETY.**

—PSALM 4:8

WHATEVER YOUR LABORS
AND ASPIRATIONS
IN THE NOISY PACE OF LIFE,
KEEP PEACE
WITHIN YOUR SOUL.

—MAX EHRMANN

THIS IS MY PRAYER:

THAT YOUR LOVE MAY ABOUND
MORE AND MORE
IN KNOWLEDGE AND DEPTH
OF INSIGHT,

SO THAT YOU MAY BE ABLE
TO DISCERN WHAT IS BEST AND
MAY BE PURE AND BLAMELESS

FOR THE DAY OF CHRIST,
FILLED WITH THE FRUIT
OF RIGHTEOUSNESS

THAT COMES THROUGH
JESUS CHRIST—TO THE GLORY
AND PRAISE OF GOD.

—PHILIPPIANS 1:9-11

STRENGTHEN US

GOD, OUR FATHER, WE ARE EXCEEDINGLY FRAIL
AND INDISPOSED TO EVERY VIRTUOUS
AND GALLANT UNDERTAKING.

STRENGTHEN OUR WEAKNESS,
WE BESEECH YOU, THAT WE MAY DO
VALIANTLY IN THIS SPIRITUAL WAR;

HELP US AGAINST OUR OWN NEGLIGENCE
AND COWARDICE, AND DEFEND US FROM THE
TREACHERY OF OUR UNFAITHFUL HEARTS,
FOR JESUS CHRIST'S SAKE.

—THOMAS À KEMPIS

THE LORD SAID TO HIM:
"I HAVE HEARD THE PRAYER AND THE PLEA
YOU HAVE MADE BEFORE ME."

—1 KINGS 9:3

DEAR LORD,

I WOKE UP TODAY.

I HAVE CLOTHES.

I HAVE FOOD.

I CAN READ.

I CAN PRAY.

I CAN LOVE.

I AM THANKFUL.

AND I AM YOURS!

THANK YOU, LORD,

FOR BEING THE ONE I PRAISE,

THE ONE WHO GIVES ME STRENGTH.

YOU ARE MY GOD,

WHO HAS PERFORMED GREAT

AND AWESOME WONDERS

THAT I HAVE SEEN WITH

MY OWN EYES.

—INSPIRED BY DEUTERONOMY 10:21

PLEASE HELP ME, FATHER,

TO PROTECT MY COMMUNITY,
CARE FOR THE POOR, FORGIVE TIRELESSLY,
AND FIGHT FOR THE POWERLESS.

MAY I SHARE MY RESOURCES,

BOTH THE SPIRITUAL AND THE PHYSICAL.
MAY I EMBRACE THE OUTCAST, AS JESUS DID.

MAY I LOVE MY GOD,

AND CHERISH THE LIFE I HAVE BEEN GIVEN.

AMEN.

—PATRICK LAWRENCE

FATHER GOD,

RIGHT NOW I NEED YOU
TO BE MY ROCK OF REFUGE,
A SAFE PLACE
WHERE I CAN GO;
PLEASE GIVE THE COMMAND
TO SAVE ME, FOR YOU ARE
MY ROCK & MY FORTRESS.
AMEN.

—INSPIRED BY PSALM 71:3

GIVE THANKS TO THE LORD,

FOR HE IS GOOD.

HIS LOVE ENDURES FOREVER.

— PSALM 136:1

PEACE I LEAVE WITH YOU;

MY PEACE I GIVE YOU.

I DO NOT GIVE TO YOU

AS THE WORLD GIVES.

DO NOT LET YOUR

HEARTS BE TROUBLED

AND DO NOT BE AFRAID.

—JOHN 14:27

MAY HE SUPPORT US
ALL THE DAY LONG,

TILL THE SHADES LENGTHEN,

AND THE EVENING COMES,

AND THE BUSY WORLD IS HUSHED,

AND THE FEVER OF LIFE IS OVER,

AND OUR WORK IS DONE!

THEN IN HIS MERCY

MAY HE GIVE US SAFE LODGING,

AND A HOLY REST,

AND PEACE AT THE LAST.

—JOHN HENRY NEWMAN

JESUS, SON OF DAVID,

PLEASE HAVE **MERCY** ON ME!

—INSPIRED BY MARK 10:47

———

WHEN ALL SEEMS LOST,

GRACE HAPPENS.

—PATRICK LAWRENCE

**HE WILL HELP THE POOR
WHEN THEY CRY OUT**

AND WILL SAVE THE NEEDY
WHEN NO ONE ELSE WILL HELP.

**HE WILL BE KIND TO
THE WEAK AND POOR,**

AND HE WILL SAVE THEIR LIVES.
HE WILL SAVE THEM FROM CRUEL PEOPLE
WHO TRY TO HURT THEM, BECAUSE
THEIR LIVES ARE PRECIOUS TO HIM.

—PSALM 72:12-14 NCV

YOU HAVE MADE US
FOR YOURSELF, O LORD,
AND OUR HEARTS ARE RESTLESS
UNTIL THEY REST IN YOU.

— SAINT AUGUSTINE

"THOUGH THE MOUNTAINS BE SHAKEN
AND THE HILLS BE REMOVED,

YET MY UNFAILING LOVE FOR YOU WILL NOT
BE SHAKEN NOR MY COVENANT
OF PEACE BE REMOVED," SAYS THE LORD,
WHO HAS COMPASSION ON YOU.

—ISAIAH 54:10

IN YOU, LORD MY GOD,
I PUT MY TRUST.

I TRUST IN YOU; DO NOT LET ME BE
PUT TO SHAME, NOR LET MY ENEMIES
TRIUMPH OVER ME.

NO ONE WHO HOPES IN YOU
WILL EVER BE PUT TO SHAME,
BUT SHAME WILL COME ON
THOSE WHO ARE TREACHEROUS
WITHOUT CAUSE.

SHOW ME YOUR WAYS, LORD,
TEACH ME YOUR PATHS. GUIDE ME
IN YOUR TRUTH AND TEACH ME,
FOR YOU ARE GOD MY SAVIOR, AND
MY HOPE IS IN YOU ALL DAY LONG.

REMEMBER, LORD, YOUR GREAT MERCY
AND LOVE, FOR THEY ARE FROM OF
OLD. DO NOT REMEMBER THE SINS OF
MY YOUTH AND MY REBELLIOUS WAYS;
ACCORDING TO YOUR LOVE REMEMBER
ME, FOR YOU, LORD, ARE GOOD.

—PSALM 25:1-7

PRAYER MAKES A GODLY MAN,

AND PUTS WITHIN HIM THE MIND OF CHRIST,

THE MIND OF HUMILITY, OF SELF-SURRENDER,

OF SERVICE, OF PITY, AND OF PRAYER.

IF WE REALLY PRAY, WE WILL BECOME MORE

LIKE GOD, OR ELSE WE WILL QUIT PRAYING.

— E.M. BOUNDS

FIRST, KEEP PEACE
WITHIN YOURSELF;
THEN YOU CAN ALSO BRING
PEACE TO OTHERS.

—THOMAS À KEMPIS

GIVE ME, O LORD, A STEADFAST HEART, WHICH NO UNWORTHY AFFECTION MAY DRAG DOWNWARDS;

GIVE ME AN UNCONQUERED HEART, WHICH NO TRIBULATION CAN WEAR OUT;

GIVE ME AN UPRIGHT HEART, WHICH NO UNWORTHY PURPOSE MAY TEMPT ASIDE.

BESTOW ON ME ALSO, O LORD MY GOD, UNDERSTANDING TO KNOW YOU, DILIGENCE TO SEEK YOU, WISDOM TO FIND YOU, AND A FAITHFULNESS THAT MAY FINALLY EMBRACE YOU, THROUGH JESUS CHRIST OUR LORD. **AMEN.**

—SAINT THOMAS AQUINAS

MY LORD GOD,

I HAVE NO IDEA WHERE I AM GOING.

I DO NOT SEE THE ROAD AHEAD OF ME.

I CANNOT KNOW FOR CERTAIN WHERE IT
WILL END.

NOR DO I REALLY KNOW MYSELF,

AND THE FACT THAT I THINK I AM
FOLLOWING YOUR WILL DOES NOT MEAN
THAT I AM ACTUALLY DOING SO.

BUT I BELIEVE THAT THE DESIRE

TO PLEASE YOU DOES IN FACT PLEASE YOU.

AND I HOPE I HAVE THAT DESIRE IN ALL
THAT I AM DOING.

I HOPE THAT I WILL NEVER

DO ANYTHING APART FROM THAT DESIRE.

AND I KNOW THAT, IF I DO THIS,

YOU WILL LEAD ME BY THE RIGHT ROAD,

THOUGH I MAY KNOW NOTHING ABOUT IT.

THEREFORE I WILL TRUST YOU ALWAYS,

THOUGH I MAY SEEM TO BE LOST AND IN

THE SHADOW OF DEATH.

I WILL NOT FEAR,

FOR YOU ARE EVER WITH ME, AND YOU

WILL NEVER LEAVE ME TO FACE MY PERILS

ALONE.

—THOMAS MERTON

LORD JESUS CHRIST,

KEEPER AND PRESERVER OF ALL THINGS,

LET THY RIGHT HAND GUARD US

BY DAY AND BY NIGHT,

WHEN WE SIT AT HOME,

AND WHEN WE WALK ABROAD,

WHEN WE LIE DOWN AND

WHEN WE RISE UP,

THAT WE MAY BE KEPT FROM ALL EVIL.

HAVE MERCY ON US SINNERS.

AMEN.

—FOURTH-CENTURY BLESSING

A PEACEFUL HEART

LEADS TO A HEALTHY BODY.

—PROVERBS 14:30 NLT

DEAR GOD,

IF I ERR THIS DAY,

MAY I ERR ON THE SIDE

OF LOVE AND MERCY.

AMEN.

GOD TO ENFOLD ME,

GOD TO SURROUND ME,

GOD IN MY SPEAKING,

GOD IN MY THINKING,

GOD IN MY SLEEPING,

GOD IN MY WAKING,

GOD IN MY WATCHING,

GOD IN MY HOPING.

GOD IN MY LIFE,

GOD IN MY LIPS,

GOD IN MY SOUL,

GOD IN MY HEART,

GOD IN MY SUFFICING,

GOD IN MY SLUMBER,

GOD IN MY EVER-LIVING SOUL,

GOD IN MY ETERNITY.

—CELTIC BLESSING

GOOD, GOOD FATHER,
REASSURE ME TODAY THAT
LOVE IS NOT WHAT I SAY;
LOVE IS WHAT I DO.
IN JESUS'S NAME, AMEN.

TRUE **PRAYER** IS NEITHER
A MERE MENTAL EXERCISE
NOR A VOCAL PERFORMANCE.
IT IS FAR DEEPER THAN THAT—
IT IS SPIRITUAL TRANSACTION
WITH THE CREATOR
OF HEAVEN AND EARTH.

—CHARLES SPURGEON

MAY THERE ALWAYS
BE WORK FOR YOUR HANDS TO DO,

MAY YOUR PURSE ALWAYS
HOLD A COIN OR TWO.

MAY THE SUN ALWAYS SHINE
UPON YOUR WINDOWPANE,

MAY A RAINBOW BE CERTAIN
TO FOLLOW EACH RAIN.

MAY THE HAND OF A FRIEND
ALWAYS BE NEAR TO YOU,

AND

MAY GOD FILL YOUR HEART
WITH GLADNESS TO CHEER YOU.

—IRISH BLESSING

IN THE MORNING, LORD,

YOU HEAR MY VOICE;

IN THE MORNING

I LAY MY REQUESTS

BEFORE YOU AND

WAIT EXPECTANTLY.

—PSALM 5:3

I KNOW NOT THE WAY
GOD LEADS ME,
BUT WELL DO I KNOW
MY GUIDE.

—MARTIN LUTHER

**IF THE HEART WANDERS
OR IS DISTRACTED,
BRING IT BACK TO THE POINT
QUITE GENTLY AND
REPLACE IT TENDERLY
IN ITS MASTER'S PRESENCE.**

—SAINT FRANCIS DE SALES

BUILD
MY LEGACY

O LORD,

OPEN MY EYES THAT I MAY
SEE THE NEEDS OF OTHERS;
OPEN MY EARS THAT I MAY
HEAR THEIR CRIES;
OPEN MY HEART SO THAT THEY
NEED NOT BE WITHOUT SUCCOR....
SHOW ME WHERE LOVE
AND FAITH ARE NEEDED,
AND USE ME TO BRING
THEM TO THOSE PLACES.
AND SO OPEN MY EYES AND
MY EARS THAT I MAY THIS
COMING DAY BE ABLE TO DO SOME
WORK OF PEACE FOR THEE.

AMEN.

—ALAN PATON

MAY MY RIGHTS BE UPHELD!

MAY MY STRENGTH BE INCREASED!

MAY MY GRAVE NOT BE DUG!

MAY DEATH NOT VISIT ME!

MAY MY JOURNEY BE FULFILLED...

MAY THE KING OF THE UNIVERSE
STRETCH TIME FOR ME!

—CELTIC PRAYER

IT SEEMED SO GREAT, MY HAPPINESS,
THAT I WAS BLESSED AND COULD BLESS.

—W.B. YEATS

DEAR JESUS,

HELP ME TO SPREAD YOUR
FRAGRANCE EVERYWHERE I GO;

FLOOD MY SOUL WITH
YOUR SPIRIT AND LIFE;

PENETRATE AND POSSESS MY WHOLE
BEING SO COMPLETELY
THAT ALL MY LIFE MAY BE ONLY
A RADIANCE OF YOURS;

SHINE THROUGH ME AND BE SO IN ME
THAT EVERYONE WITH WHOM
I COME INTO CONTACT
MAY FEEL YOUR PRESENCE WITHIN ME.

LET THEM LOOK UP AND SEE
NO LONGER ME—BUT ONLY JESUS.

AMEN.

—JOHN HENRY NEWMAN

MAY THE LORD OUR GOD BE WITH US
AS HE WAS WITH OUR ANCESTORS;
MAY HE NEVER LEAVE US NOR FORSAKE US.
MAY HE TURN OUR HEARTS TO HIM,
TO WALK IN OBEDIENCE TO HIM
AND KEEP THE COMMANDS, DECREES
AND LAWS HE GAVE OUR ANCESTORS.

—1 KINGS 8:57-58

———

WHAT COMES INTO OUR MINDS
WHEN WE THINK ABOUT GOD IS THE
MOST IMPORTANT
THING ABOUT US.

—A.W. TOZER

A FAMILY PRAYER

THANK YOU, GOD,
FOR THIS NEW DAY, FOR THE LIFE

YOU ARE GIVING
EACH MEMBER OF MY FAMILY.

BLESS EACH ONE OF US
WITH THE STRENGTH AND HEALTH

WE NEED TO SERVE
YOU TODAY, WITH THE JOY WE NEED.

MAY WE NOT GIVE IN
TO DISCOURAGEMENT, ANGER, OR BOREDOM.

GIVE US THE PROTECTION
WE NEED AGAINST PHYSICAL AND MORAL DANGER,

AND THE LOVE
WE NEED TO GIVE HOPE TO ALL WE MEET.

—AUTHOR UNKNOWN

HELP US TO SHARE YOUR BOUNTY,
NOT TO WASTE IT OR
PERVERT IT INTO PERIL

FOR OUR CHILDREN OR OUR
NEIGHBORS IN OTHER NATIONS.

YOU WHO ARE LIFE AND
ENERGY AND BLESSING,
TEACH US TO REVERE AND
RESPECT YOUR TENDER WORLD.

—THOMAS J. CARLISLE

KIDS MAY NOT REMEMBER
EVERYTHING YOU TAUGHT THEM,
BUT THEY WILL REMEMBER
HOW YOU MADE THEM FEEL LOVED.

—TAYLOR MORGAN

MAY GOD THE FATHER
WHO MADE US BLESS US.

MAY GOD THE SON
SEND HIS HEALING AMONG US.

MAY GOD THE HOLY SPIRIT
MOVE WITHIN US

AND GIVE US EYES TO SEE WITH,
EARS TO HEAR WITH, AND HANDS
THAT YOUR WORK MIGHT BE DONE.

MAY WE WALK AND PREACH THE
WORD OF GOD TO ALL.

MAY THE ANGEL OF PEACE
WATCH OVER US

AND LEAD US AT LAST BY GOD'S
GRACE TO THE KINGDOM.

—SAINT DOMINIC

MAY GOD ALWAYS WALK BESIDE YOU,

IN FRONT OF YOU, AND BEHIND YOU.

MAY HIS PEACE ABOUND IN YOUR LIFE.

MAY HIS LOVE BE YOUR ARMOR.

MAY HIS BLESSINGS SURROUND

YOU FOREVER.

MAY YOU RUN ON HOLY GROUND.

MAY YOU WALK BESIDE STILL WATERS.

— BRYCE DONOVAN

TODAY, MAY
MY MIND AND HEART
SEE ALL OF
THE GOOD IN LIFE.
AMEN.

❧

THOUGH WE TRAVEL THE WORLD OVER
TO FIND THE BEAUTIFUL,
WE MUST CARRY IT WITH US
OR WE FIND IT NOT.

— RALPH WALDO EMERSON

MAY GOD BLESS US NOT WITH
CLEAN AIR ALONE, BUT THE WILL
TO KEEP OUR AIR CLEAN.

MAY GOD BLESS US NOT WITH
A VISION OF A HEALTHY PLANET ALONE,
BUT WITH THE WILL TO DO ALL IN
OUR POWER TO RESTORE AND MAINTAIN
OUR PLANET'S HEALTH.

MAY GOD BLESS US NOT WITH
A CHANGE OF HEART IN THE GREAT
WORLD LEADERS ALONE TO SAVE
OUR PLANET, BUT WITH CHANGE IN
OUR OWN HEART TO USE OUR POWER
TO SAVE THE PLANET.

MAY THE BLESSING OF GOD NOT
BRING US TO SAINTS ALONE,
BUT MAKE OF US SAINTS GREATER
THAN ANY WE IMAGINE.

—DANIEL J. McGILL

PRAISE THE LORD.

PRAISE THE LORD FROM THE HEAVENS;

PRAISE HIM IN THE HEIGHTS ABOVE.

PRAISE HIM, ALL HIS ANGELS;

PRAISE HIM, ALL HIS HEAVENLY HOSTS.

PRAISE HIM, SUN AND MOON;

PRAISE HIM, ALL YOU SHINING STARS.

PRAISE HIM, YOU HIGHEST HEAVENS

AND YOU WATERS ABOVE THE SKIES.

LET THEM PRAISE THE NAME
OF THE LORD,

FOR AT HIS COMMAND THEY
WERE CREATED,

AND HE ESTABLISHED THEM
FOR EVER AND EVER—

HE ISSUED A DECREE THAT
WILL NEVER PASS AWAY.

—PSALM 148:1-6

MY CREATOR, I ASK FOR A
FAITH THAT MAKES ME
STRONG ENOUGH TO STAND ALONE,
WISE ENOUGH TO LIVE IN TRUTH,
AND HUMBLE ENOUGH TO ASK FOR
HELP WHEN I NEED IT.

—TAYLOR MORGAN

IN SPITE OF EVERYTHING, I STILL BELIEVE
THAT PEOPLE ARE REALLY GOOD AT HEART....
I FEEL THE SUFFERING OF MILLIONS.
AND YET, WHEN I LOOK UP AT THE SKY,
I SOMEHOW FEEL THAT EVERYTHING
WILL CHANGE FOR THE BETTER

—ANNE FRANK

SO, FRIENDS,
EVERY DAY

DO SOMETHING

THAT WON'T COMPUTE.

LOVE THE LORD.

LOVE THE WORLD.

WORK FOR NOTHING....

LOVE SOMEONE WHO

DOES NOT DESERVE IT.

—WENDELL BERRY

LORD, HELP ME TO

LOVE WHAT I HAVE

BEFORE I HAVE TO

MOURN ITS LOSS.

AMEN.

LOVE DOESN'T DIE;

PEOPLE DO.

SO WHEN ALL THAT IS

LEFT OF ME IS LOVE,

GIVE ME AWAY.

—MERRIT MALLOY

MAY THE LORD YOUR GOD LIFT YOU HIGH.

MAY YOU BE BLESSED IN THE BUSY BIG CITY
OR THE QUIET SMALL TOWN.

MAY GOD BLESS THE WORK
OF YOUR HANDS AND YOUR BRAIN.

MAY YOU BE BLESSED IN YOUR HOME,
AND FAR, FAR BEYOND YOUR HOME.

—INSPIRED BY DEUTERONOMY 28:1-12

I WILL EXALT YOU, MY GOD THE KING;

I WILL PRAISE YOUR NAME FOR EVER AND EVER...

GREAT IS THE LORD AND MOST WORTHY OF PRAISE;

HIS GREATNESS NO ONE CAN FATHOM.

ONE GENERATION COMMENDS YOUR WORKS

TO ANOTHER; THEY TELL OF YOUR MIGHTY ACTS.

—PSALM 145:1-4

LORD, BEHOLD OUR FAMILY
HERE ASSEMBLED.

WE THANK YOU FOR THIS PLACE
IN WHICH WE DWELL,

FOR THE **LOVE** THAT UNITES US,

FOR THE **PEACE** ACCORDED US THIS DAY,

FOR THE **HOPE** WITH WHICH WE
EXPECT THE MORROW;

FOR THE HEALTH, THE WORK, THE FOOD,
AND THE BRIGHT SKIES
THAT MAKE OUR LIVES DELIGHTFUL;

FOR OUR FRIENDS IN ALL PARTS
OF THE EARTH.

LET PEACE ABOUND IN OUR SMALL
COMPANY. AMEN.

— ROBERT LOUIS STEVENSON.

LET THE BELOVED OF THE LORD
REST SECURE IN HIM,
FOR HE SHIELDS HIM ALL DAY LONG,

AND THE ONE THE LORD LOVES

RESTS BETWEEN HIS SHOULDERS.

—DEUTERONOMY 33:12

A PRAYER FOR THE
CHILDREN IN MY LIFE

MAY YOU ALWAYS HOLD ON TO WHAT IS GOOD.

MAY YOU ALWAYS BELIEVE WHAT IS TRUE.

MAY YOU ALWAYS CHERISH THE LIFE YOU HAVE
BEEN GIVEN.

MAY YOU ALWAYS HOLD MY HAND, EVEN WHEN
OUR HANDS ARE FAR APART.

—BRYCE DONOVAN

GOD, WHAT DO YOU
WANT ME TO NOTICE
RIGHT NOW?
AND WHAT DO YOU
WANT ME TO DO
ONCE I HAVE TAKEN NOTE?

———

A SINGLE PRAYER CAN LAUNCH

THE ADVENTURE OF A LIFETIME.

—T.J. GORDON

DEAR GOD,
HELP ME TO REMEMBER
THAT A TRULY WISE MAN
ALWAYS SEEKS OUT
THE WISDOM IN OTHERS.
AMEN.

· · · · · · · · · ❧ · · · · · · · · ·

THE QUIET WORDS OF THE WISE
ARE MORE TO BE HEEDED
THAN THE SHOUTS OF A RULER
OF FOOLS.

—ECCLESIASTES 9:17

DEAR GOD,

AT THE END OF MY LIFE
HERE ON EARTH,

I HOPE THIS CAN BE SAID OF ME:

HE FOUGHT FOR WHAT WAS
RIGHT AND FAIR;

HE TOOK RISKS FOR THINGS
THAT MATTERED;

HE HELPED THOSE IN NEED;

HE LEFT THE EARTH
A BETTER PLACE,

BECAUSE OF WHAT HE DID,

BECAUSE OF WHO HE WAS.

—TAYLOR MORGAN

WHEN I FEEL LIKE **WORRYING,**

INSTEAD MAY I . . .

SING

SMILE

LEARN

LISTEN

HOPE

LAUGH

WORSHIP

PRAY

ENCOURAGE

LOVE.

AND **LOVE** SOME MORE.

AMEN.

— BRYCE DONOVAN

USE ME THEN, MY SAVIOR,
FOR WHATEVER PURPOSE, AND IN
WHATEVER WAY, YOU REQUIRE.

HERE IS MY POOR HEART,
AN EMPTY VESSEL.

FILL IT WITH YOUR GRACE.
HERE IS MY SINFUL AND TROUBLED SOUL.

QUICKEN AND REFRESH IT WITH YOUR LOVE.

TAKE MY HEART FOR YOUR ABODE.

MY MOUTH TO SPREAD THE GLORY
OF YOUR NAME.

MY LOVE AND ALL MY POWERS FOR THE
ADVANCEMENT OF YOUR BELIEVING PEOPLE.

NEVER ALLOW THE STEADFASTNESS
AND CONFIDENCE OF MY FAITH TO
DIMINISH—THAT AT ALL TIMES

I MAY BE ABLE FROM THE HEART TO SAY,
"JESUS NEEDS ME, AND I HIM.
SO WE SUIT EACH OTHER."

—DWIGHT L. MOODY

MAY I AND THE PEOPLE I LOVE

TREASURE THE GIFTS

YOU HAVE GIVEN US.

WE DON'T WANT YOU

TO TAKE THEM BACK.

AMEN.

———

THE EYES OF THE LORD
ARE ON THE RIGHTEOUS,
AND HIS EARS ARE
ATTENTIVE TO THEIR CRY.

—PSALM 34:15

HEAVENLY FATHER,

I AM REALIZING THAT TO MAKE

A DIFFERENCE IN MY WORLD,

I MUST DARE TO BE DIFFERENT,

ESPECIALLY WHEN THE

TRUTH NEEDS TO BE SPOKEN,

THE WORK NEEDS TO BE DONE, AND

THE HELP NEEDS TO BE OFFERED.

GIVE ME THE COURAGE,

PLEASE, TO DARE TO BE DIFFERENT.

AMEN.

— PATRICK LAWRENCE

FATHER GOD, ENABLE ME TO

CHERISH MY YESTERDAYS,
DREAM MY TOMORROWS,
AND LIVE MY TODAYS.

REMIND ME THAT TOMORROW BELONGS
TO THOSE WHO WISELY USE TODAY.
AMEN.

I CAN DO ALL THINGS THROUGH CHRIST WHO STRENGTHENS ME.

—PHILIPPIANS 4:13 NKJV

DEAR GOD,

WHEN I AM CONFUSED,

ASSURE ME THAT LIFE IS

MORE INTERESTING,

MORE INTRIGUING,

AND

MORE CHALLENGING

WHEN I DON'T HAVE

ALL THE ANSWERS.

AMEN.

INSTRUCT THE WISE

AND THEY WILL BE WISER STILL;

TEACH THE RIGHTEOUS

AND THEY WILL ADD

TO THEIR LEARNING.

—PROVERBS 9:9

THANK YOU, LORD,

FOR REFRESHING MY SOUL.

BECAUSE OF YOU, MY SPIRIT TAKES FLIGHT.

I AM HOPEFUL AND FREE

TO EXPRESS,

TO EXPLORE,

TO BE WHO YOU CREATED ME TO BE.

FOR THIS, I PRAISE YOU!

LORD, SOMEHOW, SOME WAY,
MAKE ME AN INSPIRATION
TO SOMEONE TODAY. AMEN.

COME TO ME, ALL YOU WHO ARE
WEARY AND BURDENED,
AND I WILL GIVE YOU REST.
TAKE MY YOKE UPON YOU AND LEARN FROM ME,
FOR I AM GENTLE AND HUMBLE IN HEART,
AND YOU WILL FIND REST FOR YOUR SOULS.

—MATTHEW 11:28-29

LORD, I THANK YOU FOR
THE SMALL CHALLENGES
OF DAILY LIFE.
I KNOW THEY PREPARE ME FOR
THE GREAT TESTS
OF LIFE. AMEN.

———

GOD KEEPS A FILE FOR OUR
PRAYERS—THEY ARE NOT
BLOWN AWAY BY THE WIND;
THEY ARE TREASURED IN
THE KING'S ARCHIVES.

—CHARLES SPURGEON

MAY THE GOD OF **PEACE**
BRING **PEACE** TO THIS HOUSE.
MAY THE SON OF **PEACE**
BRING **PEACE** TO THIS HOUSE.
MAY THE SPIRIT OF **PEACE**
BRING **PEACE** TO THIS HOUSE,
THIS NIGHT AND ALL NIGHTS.

—CELTIC PRAYER

YOU THEN, MY CHILD,
BE **STRENGTHENED**
BY THE **GRACE** THAT IS
IN CHRIST JESUS.

—2 TIMOTHY 2:1 ESV

MAY YOU BE STRENGTHENED
THROUGH HIS GLORIOUS MIGHT

SO THAT YOU CAN ENDURE
EVERYTHING AND HAVE PATIENCE.

MAY YOU GIVE THANKS WITH
JOY TO THE FATHER.

HE HAS ALLOWED YOU TO
TAKE PART IN THE INHERITANCE,

IN THE LIGHT THAT SHINES ON
GOD'S PRECIOUS CHILDREN.

AMEN.

—INSPIRED BY COLOSSIANS 1:11-12

ETERNAL GOD,

AS I ADJUST TO THESE
EVER-CHANGING TIMES,

HELP ME TO HOLD FIRMLY TO
UNCHANGING PRINCIPLES.

AMEN.

———

FEW WILL HAVE THE GREATNESS
TO BEND HISTORY ITSELF,
BUT EACH OF US CAN WORK TO CHANGE
A SMALL PORTION OF EVENTS,
AND IN THE TOTAL OF ALL THOSE ACTS
WILL BE WRITTEN THE HISTORY
OF THIS GENERATION.

—ROBERT F. KENNEDY

O GOD,
MAKE CLEAR TO US EACH ROAD.

O GOD,
MAKE SAFE TO US EACH STEP;

WHEN WE
STUMBLE, HOLD US;

WHEN WE
FALL, LIFT US UP;

WHEN WE
ARE HARD-PRESSED WITH EVIL,
DELIVER US; AND BRING US
AT LAST TO YOUR GLORY.

—CELTIC PRAYER

DO NOT FEAR,
FOR I AM WITH YOU;
DO NOT BE DISMAYED,
FOR I AM YOUR GOD.
I WILL STRENGTHEN YOU
AND HELP YOU.

—ISAIAH 41:10

❧

GOODNESS IS THE ONLY
INVESTMENT THAT NEVER FAILS.

—HENRY DAVID THOREAU

GIVE US GRACE

GIVE US GRACE, O GOD, TO DARE TO DO THE DEED
WHICH WE WELL KNOW CRIES TO BE DONE.

LET US NOT HESITATE BECAUSE OF EASE, OR
THE WORDS OF MEN'S MOUTHS, OR OUR OWN LIVES.

MIGHTY CAUSES ARE CALLING US—THE FREEING
OF WOMEN, THE TRAINING OF CHILDREN,
THE PUTTING DOWN OF HATE AND MURDER
AND POVERTY—ALL THESE AND MORE.

BUT THEY CALL WITH VOICES THAT MEAN
WORK AND SACRIFICES AND DEATH.

MERCIFULLY GRANT US, O GOD,
THE SPIRIT OF ESTHER, THAT WE SAY: I WILL GO
UNTO THE KING, AND IF I PERISH, I PERISH.

—W.E.B. DUBOIS

MAY GOD THE FATHER,

AND THE ETERNAL HIGH PRIEST JESUS CHRIST,

BUILD US UP IN FAITH AND TRUTH AND LOVE,

AND GRANT TO US OUR PORTION AMONG

THE SAINTS WITH ALL THOSE WHO BELIEVE

IN OUR LORD JESUS CHRIST.

WE PRAY FOR ALL SAINTS,

FOR KINGS AND RULERS....

AND FOR OURSELVES,

WE PRAY THAT OUR FRUIT MAY ABOUND

AND THAT WE MAY BE MADE PERFECT

IN CHRIST JESUS OUR LORD. AMEN.

—POLYCARP

THE GREATEST BLESSING
IN THE WHOLE WORLD
IS *BEING* A BLESSING.

—JACK HYLES

———

DEAR GOD OF ALL GENERATIONS,

AS WE POUR OUT OUR HEARTS TO YOU,

PLEASE POUR OUT YOUR GRACE ON US.

THANK YOU FOR THE GIFT OF PRAYER,

OUR SOULS' CONVERSATION WITH HEAVEN.

MAY MY FAMILY, NOW AND ALWAYS,

APPROACH YOU IN

PRAYER & WORSHIP.

—BRYCE DONOVAN

A PRAYER FOR PEACE

FONDLY DO WE HOPE,
FERVENTLY DO WE PRAY, THAT THIS
MIGHTY SCOURGE OF WAR MAY
SPEEDILY PASS AWAY. YET IF GOD
WILLS THAT IT CONTINUES. . . UNTIL
EVERY DROP OF BLOOD DRAWN WITH
THE LASH SHALL BE PAID BY ANOTHER
DRAWN WITH THE SWORD. . .

SO IT STILL MUST BE SAID:
"THE JUDGMENTS OF THE LORD ARE
TRUE AND RIGHTEOUS ALTOGETHER."

WITH MALICE TOWARD NONE; WITH CHARITY FOR ALL;

WITH FIRMNESS IN THE RIGHT, AS GOD GIVES US TO SEE THE RIGHT, LET US FINISH THE WORK WE ARE IN, TO BIND UP THE NATION'S WOUNDS;

TO CARE FOR HIM

WHO SHALL HAVE BORNE THE BATTLE AND FOR HIS WIDOW AND FOR HIS ORPHANS, TO DO ALL WHICH MAY ACHIEVE AND CHERISH A JUST AND A LASTING PEACE AMONG OURSELVES, AND WITH ALL NATIONS.

—ABRAHAM LINCOLN

A PRAYER FOR MY FAMILY

LORD, BE WITH MY FAMILY,

FROM THE OLDEST TO THE YOUNGEST.

GROW OUR RELATIONSHIPS,

GROW OUR PATIENCE,

GROW OUR LOVE,

RESTORE OUR SOULS.

SHOWER US WITH GRACE

DURING TIMES OF TROUBLE.

WEAVE LOVE INTO THE FABRIC

OF OUR FAMILY.

AMEN.

— PATRICK LAWRENCE

MAY THE LORD ANSWER YOU
WHEN YOU ARE IN DISTRESS;
MAY THE NAME OF THE GOD OF JACOB
PROTECT YOU. . . MAY HE GIVE YOU
THE DESIRE OF YOUR HEART AND MAKE
ALL YOUR PLANS SUCCEED.

—PSALM 20:1,4

PERHAPS ALL THE GOOD

THAT EVER HAS COME HERE

HAS COME BECAUSE PEOPLE

PRAYED IT INTO THE WORLD.

—WENDELL BERRY

IF I HAD A PRAYER FOR YOU TODAY,
AMONG THOSE THAT HAVE ALL
BEEN UTTERED, IT IS THE ONE WE'RE
SO FAMILIAR WITH:

"THE LORD BLESS YOU
AND KEEP YOU;

THE LORD MAKE HIS FACE
TO SHINE UPON YOU

AND BE GRACIOUS UNTO YOU;
THE LORD LIFT UP

HIS COUNTENANCE UPON YOU
AND GIVE YOU PEACE...."

AND GOD BLESS YOU ALL.

—PRESIDENT RONALD REAGAN

YOU ARE HOLY, LORD, THE ONLY GOD,
AND YOUR DEEDS ARE WONDERFUL.
YOU ARE STRONG.
YOU ARE GREAT.
YOU ARE THE MOST HIGH.
YOU ARE ALMIGHTY.

—SAINT FRANCIS OF ASSISI

PRAYER IS NOT MONOLOGUE,
BUT DIALOGUE;
GOD'S VOICE IS ITS
MOST ESSENTIAL PART.
LISTENING TO GOD'S VOICE
IS THE SECRET OF THE ASSURANCE
THAT HE WILL LISTEN TO MINE.

—ANDREW MURRAY

GOD SETS OUT THE ENTIRE CREATION

AS A SCIENCE CLASSROOM,

USING BIRDS AND BEASTS

TO TEACH WISDOM.

—JOB 35:11 MSG

———

FATHER GOD,
MAKE US CHILDREN OF QUIETNESS
AND HEIRS OF PEACE.
ENKINDLE IN US THE FIRE OF YOUR LOVE;
SOW IN US HOLY AWE FOR YOU AND YOUR CREATION.
BOLSTER OUR WEAKNESS WITH YOUR POWER.
DRAW US CLOSE TO YOU AND TO EACH OTHER
IN ONE FIRM BOND OF UNITY, TO THE GLORY
OF YOUR NAME. AMEN

—INSPIRED BY A FIRST-CENTURY LITURGY

BUT AS FOR ME, I WATCH
IN HOPE FOR THE LORD,
I WAIT FOR GOD MY SAVIOR;
MY GOD WILL HEAR ME.

—MICAH 7:7

PRAYERS OUTLIVE THE LIVES
OF THOSE WHO UTTERED THEM;
OUTLIVE A GENERATION,
OUTLIVE AN AGE, OUTLIVE A WORLD.

—E.M. BOUNDS

GRANT ME GRACE,

O MERCIFUL GOD,

TO DESIRE ARDENTLY ALL THAT

IS PLEASING TO YOU,

TO EXAMINE IT PRUDENTLY,

TO ACT IT TRUTHFULLY,

AND TO ACCOMPLISH IT PERFECTLY,

FOR THE PRAISE

AND GLORY OF YOUR NAME.

—SAINT THOMAS AQUINAS

IN THE LONG PULL, WE PRAY ONLY AS WELL AS WE LIVE.

—A.W. TOZER

❧

HEZEKIAH TURNED HIS FACE TO THE WALL
AND **PRAYED** TO THE LORD,
"REMEMBER, LORD, HOW I HAVE WALKED
BEFORE YOU FAITHFULLY AND WITH
WHOLEHEARTED DEVOTION AND HAVE DONE
WHAT IS GOOD IN YOUR EYES."

—2 KINGS 20:2-3

TIMELESS INSPIRATION.
ENLIGHTENMENT FOR DAILY LIVING.

"God shapes the world by prayer."

—E.M. BOUNDS

When you draw close to God,
God will draw close to you.

—JAMES 4:8 TLB

MAY THIS COLLECTION OF

SCRIPTURE VERSES, SPIRITUAL INSIGHTS,

AND POWERFUL PETITIONS EQUIP YOU

IN YOUR FAITH JOURNEY AND DRAW YOU

CLOSER TO GOD THIS VERY DAY.

HARVEST HOUSE
PUBLISHERS

HarvestHousePublishers.com

Prayer
ISBN 978-0-7369-8206-1

51299

9 780736 982061

U.S. $12.99